Educating Arthur

Houghton Mifflin Edition

Printed in the United States

ISBN-13: 978-0-395-92001-5
ISBN-10: 0-395-92001-9

ISBN-13: 978-0-618-93262-7
ISBN-10: 0-618-93262-3

1 2 3 4 5 6 7 8 9 VHJC 15 14 13 12 11 10 09 08

Educating Arthur

Story by Amanda Graham
Pictures by Donna Gynell

HOUGHTON MIFFLIN

Boston · Atlanta · Dallas · Geneva, Illinois · Palo Alto · Princeton

Arthur loved
chewing old slippers
for fun,
but today
there were more important
things to do.

Arthur had to help Melanie
fix her bike.

Melanie's mother needed
Arthur's help potting plants.

Arthur had to help Grandpa
bake a cake.

Grandpa wasn't sure that Arthur
was really helping at all.

"Arthur wants to help," said Grandpa,
"so let's teach him how.
Every time he does something properly,
we will give him a reward."

Arthur learned
to put his slippers away
every time Melanie said "slippers."

"Slippers, Arthur."

Whenever he did it properly,
he was richly rewarded
with a hug and a dog biscuit.

Arthur learned to tidy his basket
every time Grandpa said "tidy."
"Tidy, Arthur."

Whenever he did it properly,
he was richly rewarded
with two hugs and two dog biscuits.

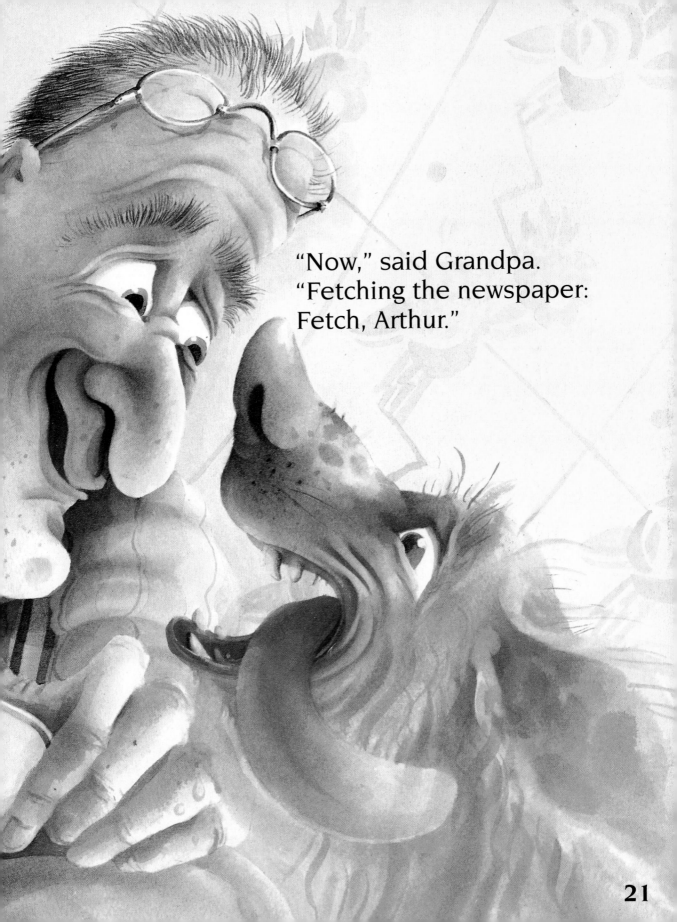

"Now," said Grandpa. "Fetching the newspaper: Fetch, Arthur."

21

It took quite some time
for Arthur to learn
to fetch the newspaper
in one piece.

But whenever
he did it properly,
he was richly rewarded
with three hugs
and three dog biscuits.

26

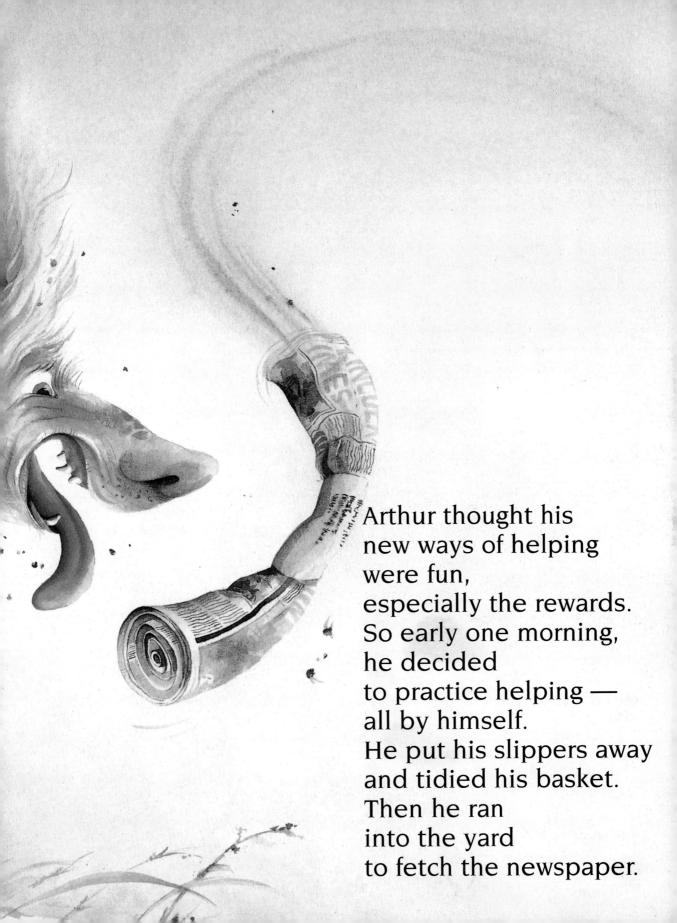

Arthur thought his
new ways of helping
were fun,
especially the rewards.
So early one morning,
he decided
to practice helping —
all by himself.
He put his slippers away
and tidied his basket.
Then he ran
into the yard
to fetch the newspaper.

Arthur went into Melanie's room
for his hugs and dog biscuits,
but she was asleep.

He went into Grandpa's room
for his hugs and dog biscuits,
but Grandpa was asleep, too.

So Arthur
collected his reward . . .

. . . all by himself!

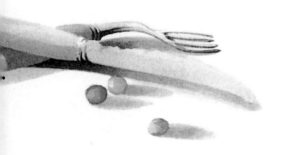